this is the book of you.

you are the author.

shine by karen brandy gunton | karenbrandy.com

copyright © karen brandy gunton 2024

ISBN 978-0-9945646-8-9

the moral rights of the author have been asserted. the suggestions and opinions of the author are personal views only. the strategies and steps outlined are a guide only. the author in all cases recommends personal due diligence and thorough research. all rights reserved. this book may not be reproduced in whole, part, stored, posted on in the internet or transmitted in any form by any means, electronic, mechanical, photocopying, recording, or other without the written permission from the author and the publisher of this book.

we each have

a light

that is all

our own

know your light

so that

you can let it

shine

to shine is

to be

who you

truly are

# this is me

look out 'cause here i come
i'm marching on to the beat i drum
i'm not scared to be seen
i make no apologies
this is me
i am brave, i am bruised
i am who i'm meant to be
this is me
i know that there's a place for us
for we are glorious
we are bursting through the barricades
and reaching for the sun
we are warriors
yeah, that's what we've become
i know that i deserve this love
there's nothing i'm not worthy of
this is brave, this is proof
this is who i'm meant to be
this is me

*from the song 'this is me'*
*performed by Keala Settle*
*written by Benj Pasek and Justin Paul*

# contents

introduction...9

22 questions to learn you...17

strengths...18

values...22

desires...26

intuition...30

spirit...34

body...38

beliefs...42

mindset...46

actions...50

emotions...54

energy...58

passions...62

purpose...66

why...70

weird...74

shadow...78

personality...82

expression...86

experiences...90

work...94

belonging...98

identity...102

conclusion...107

the lists...121

# introduction

## introduction

this is a journey of self-discovery.

a journey to know, honour, love, explore, find, remember, embrace, transform, grow, choose... BE... yourself.

as you do this work you create the book of you! it's a way to remember and honour: *this is me and who i am is brilliant!*

as we learn and deeply know ourself we build a sense of confidence, authenticity, courage, worthiness, alignment, and wholeheartedness that comes from within.

we are always changing especially as life changes around us; self-discovery and self-reflection is a time to explore and decide who we are being now.

sometimes we can experience a loss or a change in our lives that can leave us feeling lost... we've lost direction, purpose, mojo, meaning, self. self-discovery is a way to find our self and our way again.

we can also experience times where we feel dissatisfied, stagnant, stuck, unfulfilled, uncertain, unignited, or itchy... like we are longing for more. self-discovery is a way to ignite our inner light, so that we can keep shining.

know your light, learn your light... to shine is to be who you truly are.

---

SPEAK THE TRUTH. AFFIRM YOUR DESIRE. DECLARE YOUR INTENTIONS. RECALL YOUR SUCCESSES. YOUR PSYCHE WILL BELIEVE YOU. YOUR BODY WILL FEEL YOU. YOUR SOUL WILL THANK YOU FOR THE STRAIGHTUP COMMUNICATION.
- DANIELLE LAPORTE

as you go through this guidebook be kind to you. go gently, take your time, pop in and out, explore in any way you choose. it is normal to not have all the answers... the whole point is learning YOU as you go!

22 things to keep in mind as you explore YOU...

* **identity is about owning the space you are in.** it's *for you*. to know and honour yourself, to grow and transform. it's not for anyone else's comfort or agenda.

* **don't believe everything you think.** it's hard but so necessary to get really honest with yourself about the stories you tell yourself about who you think you are.

* **what other people think about you is none of your business.** other people have their own stories they are telling; these are a reflection of them, not you.

* **other people spend very little time thinking about you.** stop over estimating your importance in other people's minds, they are probably more concerned with themselves!

* **you contain multitudes.** you aren't any one thing. you are lots and lots of things. you can be so many things at once!

* **you contain nuances.** be careful of thinking only in binaries: this OR that. look for shades of grey.

* **you get to choose for yourself who you are.** identity is not up to your environment or others. choose your own labels, definitions, descriptors.

- **choose wisely.** labels can be a self-fulfilling prophecy. who you say you are is who you will be.

- **choose labels that are expansive.** ones that help you with belonging, awareness, acceptance, transformation, healing.

- **let go of labels that are constrictive.** ones that box you in, define you forever, shame you, block your growth.

- **choose what you would like to be more of.** learn it, practice it, try it on for size until it gets comfortable.

- **choose to release old labels and stories about who you are.** let it go. something you were once doesn't have to define you forever.

- **notice what you are defending.** we can sometimes hang on tightly to an identity that becomes a barrier to growth or experiencing new things.

- **the biggest cause of shame is unwanted identity.** come to peace with yucky or volatile words, definitions, labels, descriptors, and stories. aim to heal, forgive, embrace, and honour.

- **we don't often see ourselves clearly.** be real, be honest, be vulnerable, be brave, be open. when others tell you why you are brilliant, believe them!

- **question, challenge, rethink.** ask: *where does this come from? does this serve who i wish to be?* you are not here to tick boxes, you are here to explore, to peel layers, to connect dots.

* **be creative.** don't let words be another box that keeps you small, stuck, safe, and same. find new words or make up your own. write new definitions that align with who you are being.

* **get curious.** this isn't a battle. you've got nothing to win, nothing to prove. you can't fail. this is an adventure, an awakening, an exploration. ask: *i wonder what... maybe i can... what if i...?*

* **identity is not static, unchanging, concrete.** you change, especially as everything around you changes. come back to *you* again and again.

* **i like to define self as the you that is just for you.** don't just think of your self in relation to the outer world — what you offer the world, how you show up in the world, how the world sees you — **remember your inner world too!**

* **i am ___. is the most powerful sentence in the world.** you get to decide how you finish that sentence. choose wisely.

* **who you are is brilliant.** exactly as you are. i promise you this.

QUESTIONING THE PERSON YOU THINK YOU ARE
ALLOWS YOU TO UNVEIL THE PERSON
YOU ARE CAPABLE OF BECOMING
– THAIS SKY

this guidebook contains 22 questions or themes to explore, along with prompts and blank pages for brainstorming. some things to try as you explore and learn you...

* do the **quizzes** and assessments mentioned in the guidebook. you might even find some of your own!
* use the **lists** at the end of the guidebook to seek and highlight the words that fit you.
* use a **thesaurus** to find the right words when the ones you see aren't quite the right fit.
* **ask** the people who love you to help you answer the questions in this guidebook. sometimes others can help you see yourself clearly.
* use an **oracle deck** (or any other tool that helps you tune into your inner voice). sometimes these can offer clues, hints, nudges.
* write or tell a **story** about you as though you are a character in a story. sometimes 3rd person stories offer a bit of distance.
* **meditate** on a question, ask for clues or guidance. notice what shows up.
* you don't have to answer every prompt! start with the ones that **pop out** to you.
* you don't have to do this all at once or in this order! **jump in** and out, jump around, open a random page.
* **add** to this guidebook: add your own prompts, quotes, mantras, AHAs. make it yours... you are the author of the book of you!

I WILL NEVER HAVE THIS VERSION OF ME AGAIN...
LET ME SLOW DOWN AND BE WITH HER
- RUPI KAUR 'ALWAYS EVOLVING'

twenty two questions to learn you

# strengths

### what are my strengths?

strengths are gifts, abilities, skills, and talents

...it's what comes naturally to you.

while a strength can be a learned skill or ability, or it can be a natural talent or gift, the key is to explore the effect using that strength has on you.

a strength is not just something that you do because you are good at it or something that others think is good about you. your strength is something that is good *for you* to do... it strengthens you to do it.

according to positive psychology, using our strengths helps us to feel authentic, engaged, happier, and more satisfied in life.

what is your strength? something you do maybe even without realising how strong it makes you?

> A STRENGTH IS SOMETHING YOU DO THAT MAKES YOU FEEL STRENGTHENED.
> – MARCUS BUCKINGHAM

# strengths

* what do you enjoy doing so much you do it for free?

* what do people always seem to ask you for help with?

* what are you delighted to teach others?

* what seems common sense to you but is difficult for others?

* what feels like being in your zone of genius?

* what is the strength in your weakness?

* when you were little, what activities made you feel like a superhero... invincible, unstoppable, strong, ignited, in flow?

*check: strengths list page 122*
*try: free strengths test viacharacter.org*

*i am my strengths*

*i am my strengths*

# values

## what are my values?

values are fundamental ideals, guiding principles

...it's what is most important to you.

values can guide behaviour, decisions, actions and help you determine your right path. when you know what you value you can live in alignment with your values.

but values aren't just about how you show up in the outer world, your values also power your inner world, your inner self. if values had currency, then the presence of your values in any experience will add coins to your inner piggy bank. in other words, you feel powered up by what you value.

values are aspirational... they don't necessarily come naturally to you, they are something that you practice. values are action oriented... they are not goals or feelings, they are something that you do.

> WHAT IS IMPORTANT IN YOUR LIFE IS WHAT YOU DECIDE IS IMPORTANT, AND THIS DECISION WILL INDELIBLY CREATE WHO YOU ARE.
> – NEALE DONALD WALSCH

# values

* what do you wish more people would think/do/ask/care about?

* name someone important to you: someone you admire, a role model, a hero, or a beloved connection... what values to they embody?

* if you were building your ideal society/team/family from scratch, which values would be the corner stones?

* when _____ is present in any experience i feel ignited or satisfied.
  when _____ is absent from an experience i feel depleted or disappointed.

* where and for what do you use these types of phrases?
    i am certain...
    above all else...
    i won't compromise...
    i stand for...

*check: core values list page 123*
*try: free values test valuescentre.com*

i am my values

*i am my values*

# desires

## what are my desires?

desires are wishes, dreams, goals, intentions, longings

...it's what you want for you.

desires can be about what you want to have, do or achieve, where you want to go, how you want to feel, the life you want to live.

but even if you aren't sure what you want in the outer world – in the future or even right now – you can focus on your inner world, focus on the kind of person you wish to be.

you can have immediate, short term, and long term desires, and you can want different things for different parts of your life or your self, for example: work, home, family, money, health, spirit.

the things we want can change over time and can sometimes be influenced by what others want... it's always good to check back in with your desires.

ONE OF THE MOST ELOQUENT WAYS OUR SOUL SPEAKS TO US IS THROUGH OUR LONGINGS... RETURN TO YOUR LONGINGS AND THEY WILL TEACH YOU EVERYTHING. – SUE MONK KIDD

# desires

* what is your biggest dream for your self? a little dream? a future dream? an immediate dream? a secret dream?

* what brings up feelings of envy or disgust or inspiration or longing? other people can be mirrors for what we ourselves want.

* what would a perfect day look like to you?

* think back to when things were really good. what about it did you love / do you miss?

* what do you want to do/have/achieve? how do you want to feel? who do you want to be?

* what are small, easy, inconsequential things you already know you want? (remember what *yes* feels like to you!)

*check: desires + dreams lists pages 124 + 125*

*i am my desired self*

*i am my desired self*

# intuition

## how does my intuition work?

intuition is inner voice, knowing, guidance, wisdom, compass

...it's tuning into your self.

some common ways to receive messages are by feeling, seeing, hearing, knowing, sensing, or noticing a body response... but you may have another way, or a combination of ways!

watch for: "the universe/guides/angels give me messages." can you shift this to honour your inner guidance and your self as your inner guide? "my inner guide is noticing the messages in the universe... these messages are from my soul self."

when you know how your inner voice works you can build trust and faith and confidence in yourself... it's just like working a muscle that grows stronger with practice and exercise.

you listen to your intuition when you follow the path of inspiration... inspire means 'in spirit,' inspiration is a nudge from spirit.

SEEK OUT THAT PARTICULAR MENTAL ATTRIBUTE WHICH MAKES YOU FEEL MOST DEEPLY AND VITALLY ALIVE, ALONG WITH WHICH COMES THE INNER VOICE WHICH SAYS, 'THIS IS THE REAL ME,' AND WHEN YOU HAVE FOUND THAT THING, FOLLOW IT.  - WILLIAM JAMES

# intuition

* what was a time you felt tuned into your intuition? what was a time you did not listen to your intuition? what happened?

* when has someone said to you: wow, how did you know that?

* how does your inner voice signal to you? e.g. body sensations (tingles, twitches, goosebumps), pictures, words, sounds, feelings.

* what 'language' does your inner guide or soul self speak? e.g. lyrics, quotes, memes, poetry, astrology, patterns, colours.

* what sort of signs/messages/nudges/inspiration/synchronicities seem to show up in your life?

* how do you know you can trust your intuition? what might build more trust for your inner voice?

i am my intuition

*i am my intuition*

*spirit*

## how do i define my spirituality?

spirit is soul, sacred, divine, holy, cosmic, reverent

...it's what is meaningful to you.

however *you* choose to define it, understand it, and practice it.

call it what you like: god, universe, light... awakened, connected, transcendent... higher power, divinity, creator...

it's the meaningful connection to something bigger than your self, something greater than you... and not just something that is outside of you but something that is within you too.

spirit is vast and infinite... beyond any construct we can imagine. spirit is soulful and personal... it is whatever you say it is. spirit is stillness, space, and silence... requiring no words, no thought, no thing. spirit transcends... a oneness with or unity to all.

WHEREVER YOU STAND, BE THE SOUL OF THAT PLACE
- RUMI

## *spirit*

* what is your notion of who you are as divine?

* what labels and definitions do you like to use to describe your spirituality?

* what are examples of spiritual practice in your day to day life?

* what places feel holy or sacred to you?

* how do your spiritual practices and places help you connect to your divine self?

*i am my spiritual self*

*i am my spiritual self*

# body

## how embodied am i?

embodied is attuned, present, grounded, mindful

...it's your felt sense of self in the body.

to be embodied is move from the thinking mind into the feeling body, to know that your self exists in your whole body not just your mind.

to know, listen to, honour, love, embrace, celebrate your body is to know your self.

practicing embodiment can include: noticing, labelling, honouring body sensations (thirsty, tired, anxious); physical activities and movements (dancing, yoga, pottery); and sensing the environment (hot, cold, tense, calm)

all bodies are good bodies. your body is simply a vehicle – a channel or a means – for your needs, your desires, your dreams, your purpose, your work, your living of your life.

> I ALLOW THAT MY SELF IS IN MY WHOLE BODY, NOT JUST MY MIND.
> REMEMBERING MY BODY IS REMEMBERING MY SELF.
> – HILARY MCBRIDE

# body

- how embodied do you feel right now?

- in what way has it felt safe or unsafe to be your self in your body?

- how does your body communicate needs and desires with you?

- where and how are different feelings and experiences present in your body?

- how do you know, in your body, that you are content/restless, satisfied/unsatisfied, grounded/scattered, ignited/depleted, joyful/sad?

- what activities or practices help you feel embodied and/or connect to your self in your body (not just your mind).

*i am my embodied self*

*i am my embodied self*

# *beliefs*

## what do i believe?

beliefs are convictions, conclusions, ideas, theories, viewpoints

...it's what you regard as true.

but know that beliefs are not facts! all beliefs are made up... they are simply opinions and best guesses that we have embedded as true. we can let go of old beliefs and make up new beliefs!

limiting beliefs can hold you back while empowering beliefs can move you forward.

beliefs help you to make sense of the world around you and your place in it. consider what you trust, what you have faith in, what you are confident about, what you are willing to defend, and what you accept as the truth.

beliefs can and should be quite personal... if you have a belief that is based on something you've been told by others or something you have been telling yourself about a past experience, be sure to check in with how that aligns to you *now*. beliefs can and should change over time, as we learn more and experience more and open ourselves up to new perspectives our beliefs shift and change.

> YOU MIGHT NOT RECOGNISE HER NOW. SHE'S CHANGED,
> BUT NOT IN A WAY THAT'S DIFFERENT FROM HERSELF.
> IN A WAY THAT'S CLOSER TO WHO SHE IS THAN SHE'S EVER BEEN.
> THAT'S WHAT HAPPENS WHEN YOU START BELIEVING IN YOURSELF...
> YOU MEET YOURSELF ANEW.   - REBECCA RAY

# beliefs

- one thing i know to be true

- my wish for the world is

- what matters the most is

- from _____ i learned to believe that _____.

- because _____ happened i believe that _____.

- because i am _____ i believe that _____. (your strengths, values, and other qualities can impact your beliefs too!)

- a belief i am ready to shift or let go is

*check beliefs list page 126*

*i am my beliefs*

*i am my beliefs*

# mindset

## what is my mindset?

mindset is attitude, mental state, habit of mind, temperament

...it's your way of thinking.

the way you tend to approach, react, respond, handle situations and people – especially when things get hard – is based on your mindset. what you subconsciously aim to achieve in situation can also depend on your mindset (e.g. being right, liked, powerful, noticed, different.)

mindset can be positive and helpful or negative and unhelpful, and it can depend on the situation.

mindset is formed by previous experiences... it is something you can adapt and change and grow. you can work on building a growth mindset instead of a fixed mindset, an infinite mindset instead of finite, an abundance mindset rather than lack, feel impowered versus feeling like a victim, or a mindset of curiosity rather than apathy.

> BELIEVE IN YOURSELF AND ALL THAT YOU ARE. KNOW THAT THERE IS SOMETHING INSIDE YOU THAT IS GREATER THAN ANY OBSTACLE.
> – CHRISTIAN D. LARSON

# mindset

* how do you respond to challenging situations or people, when things go wrong, or when obstacles show up in your path?

* what is your best quality when under pressure? your worst?

* what situations often leave you feeling stuck?

* what does that stuckness most often look like? (e.g. procrastination, perfection, paralysis, avoid, attack, victimhood)

* describe your willingness to think about your thinking... to ask questions of yourself like *"how's that working out for me?"* or to attempt to change your thoughts/responses?

* are there any mental habits or tendencies that you'd like to adopt, shift, or release?

*try: 4 tendencies quiz quiz.gretchenrubin.com*

*i am my own mind*

*i am my own mind*

# actions

what do my actions say about who i am?

actions are behaviours, responses, states of being, verbs...

...it's what you do.

behaviour is linked to thoughts, emotions, and body sensations... what we think and feel affects what we do (and vice versa).

action is also linked to motivation in that behaviour precedes motivation... action creates momentum creates motivation! in other words, don't wait for motivation to start... motivation is created through forward, intentional action.

human behaviour is complex, unpredictable, and changeable. but knowing our 'go to behaviours' – our tendencies and patterns – as well as our different modes of action can help us to know our selves.

your actions are how you embody your identity... your actions prove your identity to yourself, or they don't. when you know who you are being you can ask: what does that type of person do?

HUMAN BEINGS ARE NOT BORN ONCE AND FOR ALL ON THE DAY THEIR MOTHERS GIVE BIRTH TO THEM... LIFE OBLIGES THEM OVER AND OVER AGAIN TO GIVE BIRTH TO THEMSELVES. - GABRIEL GARCIA MARQUEZ

# actions

* what is your common approach to taking action? (eg just do it, overthink it, procrastinate, etc)

* what is your 'go to' behaviour when you have a goal? when you are struggling? when you desire change? what other situations affect your actions?

* what strategies help you to take action? (eg investment, rewards, scheduling, mirroring, accountability buddy)

* do you have modes, rhythms, or periods of time when you have certain tendencies over others?

* what are your strengths in action? your values in action? your desires in action?

*check modes of action list page 127*

*i am my doing self*

*i am my doing self*

# emotions

## how do i feel?

emotions are states of consciousness, states of awareness

...it's how you feel.

emotions start as sensations in the body, emotions come first. feelings come next, feelings are how we consciously interpret emotions. moods develop from combinations of feelings.

the feeling self is what it means to be human. our work – part of our human experience – is to:

- tune into emotions – sense inner signals – and notice how our emotions show up on our body;
- notice, label, allow, process, and sooth our feelings (vs judging, resisting, avoiding);
- recognise and explore how our feelings affect our behaviours, beliefs, performance, decisions, communication, overcoming challenges, etc;
- build our emotional skills such as self-regulation, identifying triggers, distinguishing our emotions from others, and recognising our feelings about our feelings.

emotions are information that helps us navigate the world.

YOU ARE THE MOST TALENTED, MOST INTERESTING, AND MOST EXTRAORDINARY PERSON IN THE UNIVERSE. AND YOU ARE CAPABLE OF AMAZING THINGS. BECAUSE YOU ARE THE SPECIAL. AND SO AM I. AND SO IS EVERYONE. – EMMET, THE LEGO MOVIE

# emotions

* what is your emotional style? (e.g. feel deeply, avoid, shut down/off, fix/problem solve, apologise for, minimise, intellectualise, etc.)

* how do different emotions show up in your body? where? what types of sensations do you notice?

* what strategies help you to allow your emotions, to feel your feelings, to self-sooth or self-regulate?

* describe your sensitivity or awareness of other's emotions? how does that impact you?

* what are your feelings about your feelings - any thoughts, beliefs, rules, judgements, or stories attached to what you feel?

*i am my feeling self*

*i am my feeling self*

# energy

## how do i tend to my energy?

your energy is your fuel, bucket, battery, spark

...it's what lights you up.

some things in life will light up your spark, add fuel to your fire, or fill your bucket... they are ignitors. other things will drain your fuel, bucket, or battery, or even smother your flames... they are extinguishers.

these things can be people, places, activities, behaviours, objects, habits, energies, words, surroundings... all sorts of things!

introvert and extrovert is a common way of describing energy and what charges or drains your battery. boundaries are the steps *you* take to protect your energy (or peace)... boundaries are not what you expect others to do, they are only what you will do! you direct your own energy... where your attention goes, your energy flows.

it's important to be aware of how your energy works so that you can become a better protector of your light.

> YOU HAVE TO FIND WHAT SPARKS A LIGHT IN YOU
> SO THAT YOU IN YOUR OWN WAY CAN ILLUMINATE THE WORLD.
> – OPRAH WINFREY

# energy

* when do you feel the most energised? when do you feel the most drained? what does this feel like in your body?

* where does your energy go? what do you spend it on? does that feel like the best use for it?

* how do you most love to fill up your tank or recharge your batteries?

* what do your body, mind, soul, heart, inner child crave?

* what is your happy place? what about that place lights you up?

* how do you protect your spark, your inner flame? how do you tend to your self? honour your self?

i am my energetic self

i am my energetic self

# *passions*

## what is my passion?

passions are interests, hobbies, activities, topics, obsessions

...it's what you are really into.

passions can and do change over time... what we were once passionate about can fade for something new. but even old passions can paint a picture of who you are now as well as who you want to be!

follow the path of your passions... they can be signposts pointing to what matters most to you.

what inspires you? what excites you? what draws you in for more? what you are drawn to can point to who you want to be, where you want to go, and what you want more of next!

consider not just the thing itself that you are passionate about, but what it is about that thing that you love... *why* do you love it?

like strengths, passions aren't about what you do or offer or achieve... your passions strengthen you, they light you up from within.

THE THINGS YOU ARE PASSIONATE ABOUT ARE NOT RANDOM, THEY ARE YOUR CALLING. - FABIENNE FREDRICKSON

## passions

* what do you love doing, exploring, talking to others about?

* what did you love doing as a child?

* what have you been passionate about or always interested in over the years?

* what would you do if you had the time/money/energy?

* what are you doing when you lose track of time doing it?

* what gets you so excited that you can't sleep at night and leap out of bed in the morning?

*i am my passion*

*i am my passion*

# *purpose*

## what is my soul's purpose?

purpose is a calling, mission, intention, legacy, destiny

...it's what you are here to do.

a sense of purpose – higher purpose, life purpose, or soul purpose – gives meaning to your life... it can help with self-fulfilment, self-direction, and self-motivation.

we might think a purpose is something decided for you or planted in you – like the universe is calling you to your purpose – but actually, *you* get to choose your purpose. your true, wise self gets to make the call – that is the calling. it comes from inside you.

your primary purpose is to BE you – to remember who you were born to be – but what does that look like for you, specifically?

a purpose can be a big thing: an intention you have for the world or something you wish to accomplish in a lifetime... or it can be a little thing: something you do for you or for your everyday life or for the people around you.

a purpose is something that can help us feel a part of something that is bigger than and more important than ourselves.

your purpose is whatever you say it is.

> THERE IS NO GREATER GIFT YOU CAN GIVE OR RECEIVE
> THAN TO HONOUR YOUR CALLING. IT IS WHY YOU WERE BORN
> AND HOW YOU BECOME MOST TRULY ALIVE.   - OPRAH WINFREY

## purpose

* what do you feel called to do – or born to do – to explore, change, or talk about?

* what is that niggling thing that keeps tapping on your shoulder, trying to get your attention or nudge you in a certain direction? *try this, do this, talk about this.*

* if you were giving a ted talk or being interviewed by oprah or appearing in your favourite magazine or podcast... what would be the one message you would want to share with others?

* what would you want someone to say about you in your eulogy? what would you want your gravestone to say? *here is a person who...*

* what is one thing you'd love to do more of in everyday life (work, home, family, community) that would make life more meaningful?

* imagine someone you really admire showing up at your front door, grabbing you by the hand saying: *come on, we've got work to do!* what would that work be?

i am my purpose

*i am my purpose*

# why

## what is my why?

a why is motivation, meaning, reason, impetus, significance

...it's what drives you.

if your purpose is what you do, your why is why you do it!

your why is the thing that will keep you going, even when things get tough. your why pulls you forward to where you are going like a moth to a flame.

think about what you want, what you stand for, what matters most to you... think about who you wish to be and what you wish to do... and then ask: *why?*

keep asking *why? ok, but why? that's nice, but why? fanstastic! but why?* keep asking why until you get to the heart of what truly drives you.

a why is a way to ignite your inner light. it's not actually about the what or how or where or when or even who... but why?

DON'T ASK WHAT THE WORLD NEEDS. ASK WHAT MAKES YOU COME ALIVE AND GO DO IT. BECAUSE WHAT THE WORLD NEEDS IS PEOPLE WHO HAVE COME ALIVE.  – HOWARD THURMAN

# why

* when you're blissfully lost in the stuff you love doing, the stuff that lights you up, what is it about that stuff that drives you?

* even when things are hard, when you look like a fool or you fail, you don't give up on yourself or your dreams, why?

* there's something that's consistently mattered to you throughout your life, what is that thing and why is it important?

* what will people say about you at your funeral? what will people say is the thing that you gave to the world? what will you want to be remembered for?

* try writing 'why statements' such as:

    i believe that _____ because...
    i am here to _____ because...
    i am passionate about _____ because...
    i stand for _____ because...
    i will fight for _____ because...

*check: why + drive list pages 128 + 129*

*i am my why*

*i am my why*

# *weird*

## what makes me weird?

weird are your different, novel, quirky, goofy, odd, unusual qualities

...it's why you are one of a kind!

sometimes communities, jobs/roles, authority figures, or social constructs can put pressure on us to conform. in an effort to fit in, we become conditioned for 'normal'. our desire for belonging can make us worried about how we are perceived by others.

embrace your inner weirdness. shift your thinking from: this flaw in me/of mine, to: this flaw in culture/society. in other words: i am not broken. i don't need to be fixed. the problem isn't who i am, it's how the world views this quality.

weird often gets a negative connotation. but weird sparks creativity, curiosity, authenticity, divergent thinking, innovation, connection to others, acceptance of others. weird is awesome.

what makes you different is how you will make a difference. celebrate, honour, allow, embrace, amplify, harness your differences.

IF YOU ARE ALWAYS TRYING TO BE NORMAL, YOU WILL NEVER KNOW HOW AMAZING YOU CAN BE.   - MAYA ANGELOU

# weird

* what did people think was weird about you when you were little?

* what is weird about the people you love? admire? are drawn to? Are inspired by?

* what's something many people don't know about you?

* is there something you've dimmed down, hidden away, or tried to fix; perhaps out of fear, wanting to fit in, trying to make others more comfortable?

* what's something just a little quirky about you that you could dial up a little, amplify or harness, so that you feel wonderfully unique?

* where are the places in your life that it feels good to be a little bit weird?

*i am my weird self*

i am my werid self

# shadow

## what is hiding in my shadows?

shadow self is also known as hidden self, disowned self, dark side, inner darkness, inner demons

...it's what you don't reveal to others.

your shadow side has traits you perceive as dark, weak, unacceptable, embarrassing, or unworthy... qualities you deny, hide, abandon, or reject... consciously or unconsciously.

it includes fear, shame, guilt, doubt, worry, lack, inner critic, old wounds, and other so called negative responses or characteristics.

but your shadow side is simply a part of who you are – the flip side of the coin – because with light there is also dark.

when you shine a light of awareness into the darkness, it loses its power... when you uncover and allow and embrace all of the parts of you, you become whole, you find balance and authenticity, you heal.

be a shadow hunter, become your own flashlight, and illuminate your shadows with compassion and curiosity.

I HOPE ALL THE PARTS OF YOU THAT YOU THINK ARE HEAVY ARE PROVEN LIGHT IN MY ARMS. I HOPE THAT I CAN SHIFT AROUND THE WEIGHT YOU ARE CARRYING. I HOPE THAT I CAN MAKE YOU FEEL EASY AND WHOLE AND WORTHY.  - RACHEL CARGLE

# shadow

- what do you keep hidden away from others or wish others would never know about you?

- consider the positives of your strengths, values, personality, passions, etc… what is the dark side of that?

- what has been your biggest challenge in this lifetime? something you face over and over again or something that always seems to make you stumble?

- what do you blame others for, like least in others, or think others need to fix/change? what bothers you in others can be a disowned part of self.

- if your shadow side were to speak up right now, what would it say? what is one negative thing you say to your self? why do you hang on to that negativity?

*check: fears list page 130*

*i am my shadow self*

*i am my shadow self*

# personality

## what is my type?

personality is a collection of characteristics, qualities, traits, attributes ...it's the facets of who you are.

we often think of personality traits as dichotomous (either/or) however, don't forget that you can be more than one thing (both/and), you might be something outside of the binary (a third way), or you might be somewhere in a spectrum.

a trait might be who you naturally are or might be who you have had to be in order to manage, or maybe even who society/culture has expected you to be: a ____ kind of person as defined by the world.

a quality might be an important aspect of your true self or perhaps it does not represent your whole persona, rather it is just one part of you that you wish to honour.

you might consider personality types, archetypes, enneagram types, zodiac signs, or any other indicators of personality that you are aware of... what resonates for you?

IT TAKES COURAGE TO GROW UP AND BECOME WHO YOU REALLY ARE.
- E. E. CUMMINGS

* how would you describe your personality? think back to when you were young, what was your personality like then?

* how would others describe your personality?

* where do you feel like you perhaps had to change your personality to suit others (ex: learning to be more extraverted)

* which qualities of yours represent a just one part of you, or someone you have had to be, and which are qualities that represent your truest self or most favourite self.

* which archetypes do you most strongly identify with? are there any archetypes that you don't identify with?

* are there any other types that resonate with you (eg enneagram, zodiac, etc.)

*check: personality types + archetypes lists pages 131 + 132*
*try: free myers-briggs personality test personalitypathways.com*

*i am my many facets*

# i am my many facets

# *expression*

## how do i express myself?

expression is communication, a declaration, how you present or emphasise yourself, make a statement

...it's how you share who you are.

self-expression can include your look, style, voice, attitude, demeanour, language, movement, creativity, body language, possessions.

it's the things you say, things you do, things you have, things you know, things you care about.

your personal mode of expression can be considered your signature thing: it's what you are known for! you might already have a clear signature thing or you can be deliberate about choosing your particular signature thing(s) right now.

self-expression is sharing your insides on the outside – even if you are sharing yourself in a way that only means something to you – it helps you feel authentic, understood, seen, and in tune with your self.

IF I DON'T POKE MY HEAD OUT OF MY SHELL AND SHOW PEOPLE WHO I AM, ALL ANYONE WILL EVER THINK I AM IS MY SHELL. – SHONDA RHIMES

## expression

* what do you want to be known for? what would you say is your signature thing?

* how (and when and where) do you most love to express yourself?

* if someone saw something and thought of you, what would it be?

* if someone designed a tattoo that epitomises you, what would it be?

* how could you amplify your own self-expression... make it even more your own? how can your body be a vehicle for expression?

* in a movie about you, what would your theme song be?

* how might your inner child (or any other inner part of you) like to express them self? is there something they always wanted to try, explore, play with, wear, do, say?

*check: style + vibe list page 133*

i am my self expression

*i am my self expression*

## *experiences*

what life experiences stand out to me?

experiences are challenges, victories, turning points, AHA moments

...it's your road so far.

past experiences can shape the way we think, act, interact, respond, and experience the present. experiences can also shape how we think about our self.

own your role in your experience! instead of: __(this experience)__ made me __(brave, strong, compassionate, etc.)__ try: i made me ____, i am the gift in this experience.

try this with gratitude too! instead of: i am grateful this happened to me or for me try: i am grateful it happened because *i am me!*

our road so far can point us in the direction we go next, as long as we are willing to learn... to be curious, to look back without judgement, and to grow from wherever we have been.

COULD THERE EVER BE A MORE WONDERFUL STORY THAN YOUR OWN?<br>– NICHIREN

## experiences

* what moments from your past stand out as being important ones on your journey?

* who are the people who have had an impact in your life? whose are the voices you still hear in your head?

* what meaning have you assigned to these experiences... what story have you been telling yourself? is there a new meaning you can give to these things now?

* as you think about your life experiences what repeating patterns, recurring lessons, or turning points shaped you?

* time travel back to a moment that stands out: what would you say to or do for your past self?

* are there any ancestral experiences, family patterns, or past life memories – positive or negative – that could be having an impact on your present?

*i am my experiences*

*i am my experiences*

# work

## what is my work?

work is a job, career, vocation, occupation, enterprise, endeavour, task, project, duty

...it's how you spend your time.

your work can be paid or unpaid, at home, in a workplace, as a volunteer, as a business, for an employer, for yourself, for your family, for your community.

sometimes your work isn't as obvious as you think it is. when you think of the work you do recognise your skills as well as your contributions and include what is often unseen or what you do on the edges of what everyone thinks you do.

sometimes we can find that our role becomes our identity: i am a mom, i am a dancer, i am a doctor... being a mom/dancer/doctor is what makes me special. instead try: i am special. i make this role special. i bring something special to this role or job.

think about what YOU in particular bring to the work you do, or what you do behind the scenes, or what you do just because it brings you joy to do so... that's often the work that really matters.

YOUR WORK IS TO DISCOVER YOUR WORK AND THEN WITH ALL YOUR HEART, GIVE YOURSELF TO IT. - BUDDHA

* what tasks do you spend your time, energy, focus, and effort on?

* is there any work that you need to adjust... allow more time for YOUR best work and less time on work that others can do?

* how do you define your role? how do you make that role special?

* what do you do that only you can do? (i.e. you'd never consider outsourcing it or giving it up, the magic is in what you bring to the work or what the work gives to you.)

* what i do is _____ but what i am secretly doing at the same time/behind the scenes is _____.

* where do you get to contribute your unique brand of magic... your personal mix of passion, perspective, and potential?

* what is another name for the role you have or the work you do, something that reflects why your work is special. invent your own job title!

*check: what you do list page 134*

*i am what i bring to my work*

*i am what i bring to my work*

# belonging

## where do i belong?

belonging is community, connectedness, acceptance in a group

...it's where you get to be you.

when you think of the people, places, or activities where you belong – where you think: i belong here – try instead: here is where i am allowed to belong to myself.

think of the people and places where you don't have to adjust your self to fit in, where instead those people and places fit you... they allow you to be you and you feel more like you after time spent with them.

a community where you belong should be both a safe space and a brave space to *be you*.

true belonging fosters well-being, connection, life satisfaction, mental and physical health, feeling valued. without a sense of belonging we can feel lost, alone, disconnected, unsupported, isolated.

there is truth to the saying that we are the average of the people we spend the most time with... so choose your community wisely!

SOMETIMES THE EASIEST WAY TO FIND OUT WHO YOU ARE IS
TO BE AROUND THOSE WHERE YOU DON'T HAVE TO BE ANYTHING AT ALL.
EXCEPT YOU. AS YOU ARE. HERE NOW. – VICTORIA ERICKSON

# *belonging*

- where do you feel like you belong?

- who makes you feel safe, seen, heard, understood?

- who are the light ignitors in your world, reminding you of who you are and the light you have to shine?

- where do you feel most like you after time spent with them?

- consider the people closest to you and how those people know you; is there anything that you can honour or need to release?

- are there any spaces you dim yourself to fit in... a community that is no longer serving who you choose to be?

- for what part of your life do you wish you had a stronger community?

*i am where i belong*

*i am where i belong*

# identity

## how do i describe my identity?

identity is how you label, define, or characterise yourself

...it's how you think about you.

your identity can include: gender, sexuality, age, ability, relationships, roles, physical health, mental health, neurotype, learning, education, socioeconomics, ethnicity, race, language, religion, and so much more.

labels can be tricky; they can feel bad if they are forced on us or if we carry them around like a weight on our shoulders... but they can also be liberating if they help us to learn or understand or embrace who we are.

how you finish the sentence i am ___ matters. choose wisely! for instance, you are not your struggles... you are a brilliant person who sometimes faces struggle!

this final section is about choosing for ourselves... choosing the labels that are helpful to us and also writing our own definitions about what those words mean.

identity is not a tattoo... it's not permanent... it's fluid, shifting, changing, and adjusting. identity is not a box to keep you small and stuck, it's a liberation... a way for you to know you, to own the space you're in, to declare: *this is me.*

FOR WHAT IT'S WORTH: IT'S NEVER TOO LATE OR TOO EARLY TO BE WHOEVER YOU WANT TO BE. YOU CAN CHANGE OR STAY THE SAME, THERE ARE NO RULES TO THIS THING. I HOPE YOU LIVE A LIFE YOU'RE PROUD OF. IF YOU FIND THAT YOU'RE NOT, I HOPE YOU HAVE THE COURAGE TO START ALL OVER AGAIN.
– ERIC ROTH

* what labels do you choose to use for yourself?

* what definitions do you choose to use for yourself?

* what helps you to describe, own, honour, embrace, and/or remember who you are?

* are there any labels or definitions you need to discard as they no longer work for you or reclaim, take back, and make yours?

* are there any "i am" statements you wish to adjust (eg i am depressed vs i am a deeply feeling sensitive soul who experiences depression sometimes)

* are there any other themes or identifiers that haven't been covered in this guidebook that you still wish to explore, define, embrace? add more of your labels here!

*i am my chosen identity*

*i am my chosen identity*

# conclusion

*conclusion*

now what? you've learned and honoured and embraced and explored all of these amazing and interesting things about you. what do you do with that information?

**layer it all together.** all of it paints a picture of who you are and all of it together makes you 100% unique and amazing! you aren't any one thing, you are a collection of many things, of ALL the things.

the title of this guidebook is *shine* to remind you that you that you have a light that is all your own.

if you think of that light as a rainbow, know that it is made up of many colours, many layers. or perhaps you might like to think of your light as a chandelier made up of many brilliant facets or a string of tiny lights connected together to shine bright.

there are other ways to think in layers: perhaps you think of you as a stunning spiral staircase, or a beautiful rainbow layer cake, or a matryoshka nesting doll... layers and layers of things that together make you you!

or maybe instead you are a cheetah with a unique pattern of spots that no one else has, or a painting with many shades and colours, or a puzzle with a variety of pieces... some you might not have even discovered yet!

this book is your space to paint those colours, connect those lights, build those layers... to shine brilliantly as you are.

YOU ARE UNREPEATABLE. THERE IS A MAGIC ABOUT YOU THAT IS ALL YOUR OWN.  – D.M. DELLINGER

*this is me*

* what are some of the key things you want to remember, honour, embrace, or amplify about you?

* did you notice any trends, patterns, or themes as you worked through the 22 questions in this guidebook?

* are there any dots that you can connect, or puzzle pieces you can click together, or layers you can add to this picture you have of who you are?

* was there anything you noticed about you that you had forgotten or hidden or lost along the way? anything you learned that is really amazing that you want to celebrate? anything that you have decided you want to be more of?

* what makes you *you*? what makes *your* light shine?

i am me

*i am light*

# conclusion

## i am enough

now that you have honoured all of the brilliant layers that together make you who you are, use this knowledge – this evidence – to always remember that...

**who you are is exactly, wonderfully, perfectly enough. just as you are.**

your value is inherent. it is in all of the things that make you you. no one else on earth has the exact combination of colours and layers and pieces and shades as you do... your light is brilliant, it is needed, it is enough, it matters.

you are worthy and deserving of a life that lights you up inside. you do not need to change who you are, you do not need to put on a persona or be who anyone else thinks you ought to be, you do not need to hide or dim or make yourself small.

when you walk into a room, when you stretch out of your comfort zone, when you go after your dreams... remember you are worthy exactly as you are. be empowered simply by being you.

whatever you may be seeking, the thing you are looking for – self-worth, self-confidence, courage, drive, purpose, acceptance, transformation – know that it is in you already. it is of you.

celebrate your largeness, your magnitude, your brilliance. you are complex, unique, grand, whole, worthy. you were born to be you. you were born to shine. this is your gift.

LIFE'S MAGIC WORKS THROUGH YOU. NOT BESIDE YOU. NOT AROUND YOU. NOT FOR YOU. NOT INSTEAD OF YOU. THROUGH YOU.  – MIKE DOOLEY

# *conclusion*

## i am whole

just as this work reminds you of your enoughness, let it also remind you of your wholeness. you are not broken or defective or damaged goods.

**who you are is perfectly imperfect.**

sometimes the world can make us feel like we need to fix or solve or adjust or correct or uplevel or improve or overcome or erradicate the imperfect parts of our selves... like who we are is a problem.

sometimes our struggles make us feel like there is something wrong with us... we think that we should be better or do better, that we should get over it or move on by now or have solved that already... like who we are is *the* problem.

these messages can make us question who we thought we were... our sense of self gets rocked and we feel even more stuck!

learning how you shine is not just about knowing your self, it's about treating yourself not as a problem to be fixed but as a human be-ing... a self becoming.

when the world tells you to fix or uplevel or get over, please pause and let that message go. instead, practice leaning in, allowing, embracing, and honoring your struggling, imperfect self.

to be flawed, to be struggling, is to be human.

TO BE YOURSELF IN A WORLD THAT IS CONSTANTLY
TRYING TO MAKE YOU SOMETHING ELSE IS THE GREATEST
ACCOMPLISHMENT  - RALPH WALDO EMERSON

# conclusion
## self + parts

it can be helpful to think of ourselves as having both a SELF (our inner self, true self, wise self) and parts. you might already do this by thinking of your inner child or inner critic... you can expand this and consider you may have an inner rebel, people pleaser, hermit, bossy pants, or rock star. you might think of some of your archetypes, personality types, tendencies, roles, shadow aspects, or other qualities as parts.

when we are struggling or stuck, those parts may be agitated, activated, sabotaging, or suffering in some way... so do keep in mind that **it is not your whole self who is struggling, it's just one part.**

this is the remarkable power of the self! every thing we do to strengthen our sense of self will help us to alleviate struggle. self is the prerequisite to healing, shifting, growing, thriving... shining!

the concept of parts can also help us to practice self-compassion... we can treat our parts as valued members of team SELF, which they are! there are no bad parts, your parts only want to keep you safe or help you in some way.

we can turn towards our struggling parts... we can accept and allow their experience... we can give them a big hug of thanks... and then we can engage our true SELF to be the one who leads us forward out of stuckness and toward more of what we really want.

I CANNOT BE THE LEADER I AM MEANT TO BE WITHOUT ALL OF THE PARTS OF WHO I AM.   - AMERICA FERRERA

# conclusion

## acceptance + equality

just as you are brilliantly special and unique as you are, thanks to all the layers that make you you, so is everyone else.

**each of us has our own brilliant light to shine, in any way we choose.**

we cannot always understand how others choose to or are born to live... to express, to relate, to work, to play, to explore, to rise, to shine. just as you have your own labels and definitions and identity... so do others, in just as unique and beautiful a combination as yours.

as you do the work to honour and embrace and accept *yourself*, let this also be an invitation to honour *others*. their identity is just as valid, as worthy, and as amazing as yours is.

when you find yourself uncomfortable with, confused about, or unaccepting of another person's identity – if someone shares the truth of who they are and you judge or minimise or disregard them – please pause and ask: what insecurities do you have about your own sense of who you are that feels threatened by someone else's identity?

do the work to know and accept yourself so that you can be more accepting of others. you don't have to *get* another person's identity, based on your understanding of the world, in order to offer acceptance. we are all deserving of acceptance, just as we are.

> I LEARNED THAT ACCEPTING OTHERS AND ACCEPTING MYSELF ARE TWO SIDES OF THE SAME COIN; YOU CAN'T LOVE AND ACCEPT YOURSELF WITHOUT DOING THE SAME FOR OTHERS. - STEVE PAVLINA

# conclusion
### i will keep learning me

now that you know who you are being, what can you be doing? what is the next step for you?

your work in self-discovery, self-honouring, and self-love is never done. **become a lifelong seeker, be a learner at the university of YOU.**

stay curious... keep questioning, challenging, and re-thinking. stay open... to the world around you and also the world within you. it's always your choice... to choose who you are being and to give yourself permission to shine.

there may be questions in this guidebook that you feel you can't answer, that feel hard or even scary. these things are actually clues... they point to places where you can give yourself permission, forgiveness, healing, compassion, or exploration. this is simply about knowing yourself and being yourself... it's why we are here! so give yourself heaps of self-love and come back to it!

if a time comes when you feel lost, when you doubt your worth, when you experience a change, when your identity shifts in some way, when you feel stuck, or you feel a bit itchy like you are ready for your next chapter... come back to this guidebook... come back to you. come back again and again.

to know your light is to shine even brighter.

A SELF IS NOT SOMETHING STATIC. TIED UP IN A PRETTY PARCEL FINISHED AND COMPLETE. A SELF IS ALWAYS BECOMING. – MADELEINE L'ENGLE

# conclusion
## other lessons to remember

# i am me

i strengthen myself with my strengths

i activate myself with my values

i cultivate myself with my desires

i listen to myself with my intuition

i expand myself with my spirituality

i embody myself with my body

i know myself with my mindset

i empower myself with my beliefs

i act like myself with my actions

i allow myself with my feelings

i honour myself with my energy

i explore myself with my passions

i fulfill myself with my purpose

i ignite myself with my why

i amplify myself with my weird

i embrace myself with my shadows

i recognise myself with my personality

i share myself with my expression

i appreciate myself with my experiences

i contribute myself with my work

i get to be myself with my belonging

i liberate myself with my identity

# i am light

i am light, i am light, i am light

i am not the things my family did
i am not the voices in my head
i am not the pieces of the brokenness inside

i am light, i am light, i am light

i am not the mistakes that i have made
or any of the things that caused me pain
i am not the pieces of the dream i left behind

i am light, i am light, i am light

i am not the colour of my eyes
i am not the skin on the outside
i am not my age
i am not my race

my soul inside is all light

all light, all light, all light

i am light, i am light, i am light

i am divinity defined
i am the god on the inside
i am a star
a piece of it all

i am light

*from the song "i am light'*
*written and performed by india arie*

*the lists*

# strengths

| | | |
|---|---|---|
| accuracy | forceful | outgoing |
| action oriented | friendliness | patient |
| adventurous | generosity | perseverance |
| ambitious | gratitude | persuasiveness |
| analytical | helpfulness | persistence |
| appreciative | honesty | practical |
| artistic | hope | precise |
| athletic | humility | problem solving |
| authentic | humour | prudence |
| bold | idealism | respect |
| caring | independence | responsibility |
| clever | ingenuity | self-assurance |
| compassionate | industriousness | seriousness |
| charming | inner peace | self-control |
| communicative | inspirational | spirituality |
| confident | integrity | spontaneous |
| considerate | intelligence | social intelligence |
| courage | kindness | social skills |
| creativity | knowledgeable | straightforward |
| critical thinking | leadership | strategic thinking |
| curiosity | lively | tactful |
| dedication | logical | team oriented |
| determination | love | tenacious |
| discipline | love of learning | thoughtful |
| educated | mercy | thrifty |
| empathetic | modesty | tolerant |
| energetic | motivation | trustworthy |
| entertaining | observant | versatile |
| enthusiastic | optimistic | visionary |
| fair | open minded | vitality |
| fast | orderly | warmth |
| flexible | originality | willpower |
| focused | organization | wisdom |

# values

- adventure
- balance
- beauty
- calm
- challenge
- change
- commitment
- communication
- community
- competence
- connection
- consistence
- creativity
- education
- efficiency
- effort
- equality
- excellence
- fame
- family
- fitness
- freedom
- friendship
- fun
- generosity
- growth
- health
- honesty
- humour
- independence
- individualism
- influence
- innovation
- intellect
- joy
- kindness
- knowledge
- leadership
- love
- loyalty
- money
- open-mindedness
- order
- peace
- personal expression
- personal growth
- privacy
- recognition
- safety
- service
- significance
- simplicity
- spirituality
- stability
- truth
- well being

# desires

| | | |
|---|---|---|
| adventurous | enriched | positive |
| affectionate | euphoric | prominent |
| aligned | exhilarated | prosperous |
| alive | fierce | pure |
| anchored | focused | refreshed |
| appreciative | fortunate | renewed |
| attentive | free | resilient |
| auspicious | fruitful | safe |
| authentic | fulfilled | secure |
| awake | generous | serene |
| balanced | genius | significant |
| beautiful | gifted | soft |
| belonging | guided | soulful |
| bold | harmonious | spiritual |
| boundless | healed | spontaneous |
| brilliant | healthy | steady |
| captivated | hypnotic | strong |
| celebrated | illuminated | sultry |
| centred | independent | supported |
| certain | influential | sure |
| charismatic | inspired | thoughtful |
| clear | intentional | trailblazing |
| confident | inviting | transformed |
| connected | joyful | treasured |
| courageous | kind | triumphant |
| curious | love | unconditional |
| deep | loyal | unshackled |
| deserving | luxurious | untamed |
| devoted | magnetic | useful |
| direct | miraculous | vast |
| elevated | natural | visible |
| embraced | nurtured | wealthy |
| emergent | open | whole |
| empowered | pampered | wild |
| engaged | pleasure | wise |
| enlightened | poetic | worth |

# dreams

have purpose to my life
do it right, be right, make right decisions/choices
know/trust what is best for myself
have a voice, be heard
be respected
be appreciated
be trusted
be popular
be successful
people agree with me
in control of my life
have security
be able take care of others
know i will be taken care of
make an impact
leave something behind (a legacy)
get noticed
reach a goal
have more freedom
have more flexibility
feel fulfilled

feel empowered
feel loved
feel complete/whole
happiness/joy/bliss/passion
health
wealth
certainty – everything will be ok
connected – not alone
clarity - know exactly what to do
simplicity
ease
comfort
longevity
status
luxury
lifestyle
do the thing always wanted to do
do the thing longing to do
do what i love

# beliefs

## limiting beliefs:

i am not ___ enough
i don't have enough ___
i am too ___
i can't ___ because ___
i need to ___ before i can ___
i don't know ___
it's not possible to ___
i'm not ready to ___
i don't deserve to ___
they think i ___
i will never ___
i will always ___
i will lose ___ if i ___

i will fail
i will be judged
i will disappoint
why bother
it's too late
it's too hard
it's too scary
it's selfish
it's a waste of time
i should
i shouldn't
this is just who i am
this is how things will always be

## empowering beliefs:

i can't ___ YET
i can
i have
i know
i choose
i practice
i embrace
i challenge
i accept
i ask
i try
i allow
i am willing
i am ready

i am learning
i am worthy
i am supported
i am free
i am curious
i am stronger than i think
i am here for a reason
i have so much to offer
it is possible
it is safe
it is ok to ___
i take responsibility for ___
i believe in myself

## modes of action

| | |
|---|---|
| risktaker | doer/JFDI |
| risk adverse | watcher/learner |
| optimist | thinker/contemplator |
| pessimist | talker/analyser |
| second guesser | self-motivated |
| trendsetter | externally-motivated |
| innovator | spontaneous |
| early adopter | scheduler |
| rebel | scheduler |
| rule follower | goal setter |
| leaper | routine lover |
| baby stepper | results driven |
| cautious | reward driven |
| careful | accountability driven |
| meticulous | investment driven |
| efficient | permission seeker |
| planner | forgiveness seeker |
| list maker | procrastinator |
| dreamer | hyper focused |
| leader | easily distracted |
| follower | multi tasker |
| laggard | go-getter |
| delegator | workhorse |
| micromanager | workaholic |
| perfectionist | busy bee |
| imperfectionist | sloth |
| work in progress | ask for help |
| overachiever | do it by my self |
| overthinker | do it my way |

# why + drive

| | | |
|---|---|---|
| accuracy | connection | extravagance |
| achievement | continuity | fairness |
| action | control | faith |
| activeness | conviction | fame |
| advancement | cooperation | family |
| adventure | courage | fidelity |
| affection | creativity | fitness |
| affluence | decisiveness | fortitude |
| altruism | delight | freedom |
| ambition | depth | friendship |
| analysis | determination | fun |
| approval | development | generosity |
| balance | devotion | grace |
| beauty | dignity | gratitude |
| belonging | discipline | gratitude |
| benevolence | discovery | growth |
| bliss | diversity | guidance |
| boldness | dominance | happiness |
| bravery | drive | harmony |
| brilliance | duty | health |
| candour | ease | helpfulness |
| carefulness | education | honesty |
| celebrity | efficiency | honour |
| challenge | elegance | humility |
| change | empathy | humour |
| charity | encouragement | imagination |
| cheerfulness | energy | inclusiveness |
| clarity | enjoyment | independence |
| cleanliness | entertainment | individuality |
| comfort | enthusiasm | influence |
| commitment | environmentalism | ingenuity |
| community | ethics | innovation |
| compassion | excellence | inquisitiveness |
| competence | excitement | insightfulness |
| competition | expertise | inspiration |
| confidence | exploration | integrity |

# why + drive

| | | |
|---|---|---|
| intelligence | passion | security |
| intensity | peace | security |
| intimacy | perfection | self-control |
| introspection | perseverance | selflessness |
| introversion | philanthropy | self-respect |
| justice | playfulness | serenity |
| kindness | popularity | service |
| knowledge | positivity | silence |
| leadership | potential | simplicity |
| learning | power | solidarity |
| legacy | practicality | solitude |
| liberty | pragmatism | spirituality |
| logic | precision | spontaneity |
| longevity | preparedness | spunk |
| love | pride | stability |
| loyalty | privacy | strength |
| mastery | problem-solving | structure |
| maturity | professionalism | surprise |
| meaning | progress | sympathy |
| meticulousness | punctuality | teaching |
| mindfulness | reason | teamwork |
| modesty | recognition | thoroughness |
| mystery | recreation | thrill |
| nature | relaxation | transparency |
| neatness | reliability | trustworthiness |
| nonconformity | religion | uniqueness |
| obedience | reputation | variety |
| open-mindedness | respect | vision |
| optimism | responsibility | volunteering |
| order | rest | warmth |
| organization | risk-taking | wealth |
| originality | sacredness | willingness |
| outdoors | sacrifice | wisdom |
| outrageousness | satisfaction | wonder |
| partnership | science | youthfulness |

# fears

| | |
|---|---|
| not good enough | not being approved of |
| won't ever measure up | never having enough money |
| failure | something will go wrong |
| lose money | people will hate it |
| lose face | people will hate me |
| too hard | it won't work |
| don't know what to do | making the wrong decision |
| can't do it | rejection |
| not perfect | being judged |
| not worthy | getting hurt |
| not deserving | too late |
| why bother | missed my chance |
| who am i to do this? | looking foolish |
| be found out | disappointing someone |
| no one will care | wasting time |
| do the wrong thing | losing money |
| turn people off | losing love |
| piss people off | having nothing |
| make a huge mistake | not being liked |
| it's too easy so it must be wrong | something bad will happen |
| can't compete | something wrong with it/me |
| waste of time | don't belong here |

# personality type

imaginative v. practical

worried v. confident

dominant v. submissive

calm v. high-strung

spontaneous v. restrained

flexible v. resistant

controlled v. undisciplined

closed off v. open

abstract v. concrete

conforming v. non-conforming

self-sufficient v. dependent

tender-hearted v. tough-minded

uninhibited v. shy

impatient v. relaxed

suspicious v. trusting

outgoing v. reserved

extraversion v. introversion

sensing v. intuition

thinking v. feeling

judging v. perceiving

# archetypes

| | | |
|---|---|---|
| actor | innocent | prophet |
| addict | investigator | puck |
| artist | jester | rebel |
| alchemist | judge | revolutionary |
| adventurer | knight | redeemer |
| anarchist | liberator | robot |
| achiever | lover | rescuer |
| beggar | magician | romantic |
| bureaucrat | matriarch | ruler |
| caregiver | masochist | saboteur |
| challenger | mediator | samaritan |
| companion | monk | sage |
| crone | muse | scribe |
| child | martyr | seer |
| clown | midas | shaman |
| creator | mystic | sage |
| damsel | networker | scout |
| diva | olympian | seeker |
| dictator | orphan | settler |
| disciple | observer | slave |
| detective | peacemaker | student |
| diplomat | protector | scholar |
| dreamer | pioneer | seductress |
| fool | princess | servant |
| evangelist | provocateur | sidekick |
| explorer | puritan | storyteller |
| gambler | pilgrim | teacher |
| giver | politician | trickster |
| goddess | prince | thief |
| herald | prostitute | tyrant |
| healer | puppet | warrior |
| helper | patriarch | visionary |
| hero | perfectionist | victim |
| historian | performer | witch |
| hermit | poet | wizard |
| innovator | priest | |

# style + vibe

| | | | |
|---|---|---|---|
| accessible | custom | innovative | risk-taking |
| accurate | cute | inspiring | romantic |
| adaptable | cutting-edge | intellectual | safe |
| adorable | dangerous | intimate | secure |
| affordable | deep | intuitive | sensitive |
| agreeable | determined | irresistible | serious |
| alternative | diligent | kind | smart |
| ambitious | dreamy | knowledgeable | soft |
| antique | dynamic | light-hearted | solid |
| artistic | earthy | lively | soulful |
| assertive | ease | luxurious | spacious |
| bespoke | easy-going | masculine | speedy |
| bold | edgy | minimalist | spiritual |
| bright | elegant | modern | state-of-the-art |
| calming | enthusiastic | natural | strategic |
| candid | environmental | no-frills | successful |
| cheap | ethereal | old-school | surprising |
| cheeky | excellence | original | sustainable |
| cheerful | expert | outrageous | sweet |
| childlike | fast | passionate | timeless |
| classic | fearless | playful | tough |
| classy | flexible | positive | traditional |
| clean | fun | powerful | trendy |
| clever | funky | pragmatic | trustworthy |
| comfortable | funny | premium | uncluttered |
| competitive | gentle | professional | unexpected |
| confident | glamorous | punctual | unique |
| conservative | grounded | quality | value-added |
| controversial | harmonious | quick | wacky |
| conventional | healthy | quirky | warm |
| co-operative | heart-centred | relaxed | whimsical |
| corporate | helpful | reliable | wild |
| cozy | honest | remarkable | zen |
| crafty | hopeful | responsible | |
| current | humorous | rigid | |

# what you do

**you do things. offer a service.**

| | | | |
|---|---|---|---|
| analyst | facilitator | master | revolutionary |
| connector | guru | moderator | specialist |
| coordinator | identifier | partner | stylist |
| dynamo | magician | practitioner | tweaker |
| expert | manager | promoter | visionary |

**you share things. provide expertise.**

| | | | |
|---|---|---|---|
| advisor | explorer | leader | strategist |
| coach | guide | mastermind | teacher |
| consultant | healer | mentor | therapist |
| director | instructor | muse | trainer |
| educator | intuitive | pathfinder | tutor |

**you make things. create a product.**

| | | | |
|---|---|---|---|
| architect | author | developer | inventor |
| artisan | builder | entertainer | maker |
| artist | craftsperson | fabricator | producer |
| artiste | creator | generator | scribe |
| assembler | designer | handmaker | writer |

**you source things. sell a product.**

| | | | |
|---|---|---|---|
| advocate | curator | fiend | keeper |
| aficionado | dealer | founder | launcher |
| buff | defender | galvanizer | lover |
| collector | devotee | influencer | proponent |
| connoisseur | enthusiast | junkie | seeker |

**you aid things. give assistance.**

| | | | |
|---|---|---|---|
| advocate | benefactor | encourager | planner |
| aide | champion | helper | provider |
| assistant | cheerleader | nurturer | refiner |
| associate | companion | organiser | representative |
| attendant | contributor | patron | supporter |

# other

## about the creator

karen brandy gunton is an author, teacher, and life coach with a focus on self-development and self-empowerment. she is on a mission to get unstuck and do more of what lights her up.

she is also badass rule-breaker who never uses capitals because she lives her own message, which is permission to be you... to own your light and shine your way.

karen is a canadian girl who lives in adelaide, australia with her husband, her three children, and her two demotivational support frenchies. you can find her in her happy place on the beach with a book in one hand, a cold beer in the other, and her bare toes in the sand.

find karen on instagram @karenbrandy or at her website karenbrandy.com

## find more

### enough.

a free ebook. now that you have done the work to learn you... choose you! claim your self. claim your worth. beacuse you deserve your favourite version of life!

### rise.

55 simple self-leadership strategies to get unstuck or make a change.

### illuminate.

77 card oracle deck + guidebook... explore your inner voice and inner guidance.

visit the bookshop at karenbrandy.com

www.ingramcontent.com/pod-product-compliance
Lightning Source LLC
Chambersburg PA
CBHW061153010526
44118CB00027B/2963